VENUS EXAM

POETRY BY MAUREEN SEATON

The Sea among the Cupboards
Fear of Subways
Furious Cooking
Exquisite Politics (with Denise Duhamel)
Little Ice Age

CHAPBOOKS

Miss Molly Rockin'
Oyl (with Denise Duhamel)
Little Novels (with Denise Duhamel)

VENUS EXAMINES HER BREAST

POEMS BY
MAUREEN SEATON

CARNEGIE MELLON UNIVERSITY PRESS
PITTSBURGH 2004

ACKNOWLEDGMENTS

Many thanks to the editors and staffs of the following journals in which these poems first appeared, some in earlier versions:

ACM: "The Girls of Doom," "St. Lucie," "Toy Weather 3"
Carnegie Mellon Poetry Review: "Fay Wray," "π," "Sentencing"
Columbia Poetry Review: "She Sat in My Lap Like a Stone"
Crab Orchard Review: "Pilgrimage to Bethlehem Steel"
Crowd: "Bijou"
Denver Quarterly: "You're Babylon and I'm Brazil"
Folio: "A Glossary of Fog," "Pele," "Questions for an Outlaw," "Turtle Beach"
Green Mountains Review: "He Crossed the Hallway with a Soul in His Hand"
Indiana Review: "Interview with Bonnie Parker," "Realm of the Wide"
Provincetown Arts: "Venus Examines Her Breast"
Quarter After Eight: "Red," "Riding Hood," "Toy Weather 2," "The Possible," "Worm Reef"
Rhino: "Toy Weather"
TriQuarterly: "Eating Florida"

Sections of "Red" and "Toy Weather 2" were collaged and reprinted in *ChaoSity*, an e-book/website co-authored with Niki Nolin, Karen Lee Osborne and Wade Roberts, through a grant from Columbia College Chicago, 2000. "Toy Weather," along with *Rhino*, won a 2002 Illinois Arts Council Literary Award. "π" was reprinted in the libretto by Denise Duhamel for "Queen Bee-ing," an opera by Sorrel Hays (Medicine Show, NYC, June 2003). "Turtle Beach," "Eating Florida," "Worm Reef," and "St. Lucie" were reprinted in *Tigertail: South Florida Poetry Annual*.

Book design: Connie Amoroso
The publication of this book is supported by a grant from the Pennsylvania Council on the Arts.

PENNSYLVANIA COUNCIL ON THE

Library of Congress Control Number: 2003103593
ISBN 0-88748-408-5

10 9 8 7 6 5 4 3 2 1

ARTS

FOR MARICE

(1926—1999)

CONTENTS

PILGRIMAGE TO BETHLEHEM STEEL

Even when you say it—*Stop*—
something requires movement, something

the heft and seize of stillness, a cameo
centered at bare throat, held in the palm,

fact of silver, something small to munch on.
This chill is how air feels to the dying,

the way the dead do magic on your dashboard,
their tricks unappreciated, their finesse

ignored. The trick of suffering
is suspense. Without it you'd glide—

white scarf in a snowstorm, flower
called *violet* in your suit's lapel.

I went to a funeral once and had fun.
We sang loud and became foolish

on the deceased's favorite highball. We
bunny-hopped around the casket,

patted each other into glowy remembrance.
To be honest, I saw that wake in a movie.

I laughed so hard the masturbator in the next row
fled. Now stand in a circle on the lip

of Lake Michigan, sunset, a few feet
from the dangerous ice shelf, facing North.

Pretend the four elements of life
arrive at your bidding. Hold driftwood, say:

The sun gives glory to the steel mills and
Bethlehem's gorgeous in the dying light.

★

RED

(i)

Whenever we admire ourselves we admire ourselves to the sound
        of the train to the metal
doo-wopping to the grind and the slowing down of squeak and bend,
        stop and gorgeous start.

Remember when everything was tight and we were pointy
        because our shoes made noise
and our shoes made noise and our shoes made noise?

We showed off like flowers, those hyperboles, strolled down the path
        in time to "Walk
Away, Renée," slowed behind ambulances, police cars at angles,
        still figure on macadam.

I don't know if she'd been hit by a car or if fate had come along
        and touched her nose.
Tweak, said Fate. Sweet bird-noise, silk of a poppy's petal.

(ii)

I flew across the land toward what seemed like a vast sea of females
        roaring macroscopically
along the shore of Chicago. I saw a dead woman on the street
        and I was the dead woman.

I woke to the smell of tea which the woman had poured before
        the dream. My
computer was sleeping and I was my computer. I was about to have sex
        with the Wizard.

(iii)

"Ah," she said, like an oracle. I used so many words in a row
        my line slid off the page.

It was the way it sprang back that seemed precocious, no,
          ferocious, no,

strangely jelly-like as if frozen to the backs of spoons and dipped
          into a holy water font.

I was holding a baby in my arms. As we passed the font, she
          leaned down and dipped
her hand into the dirty water then into her mouth. Mmm, she said,
          her baby eyes shining.

(iv)

We built buildings to walk us skyward. The way a single leaf, then
          a whole tree but reversed.
There were always people with edges and hostilities, glut and paranoia.
          I walked around

and into and through and sometimes on or beyond. Before prepositions
          life
was a scene of wildflowers. Fire and desire. Conflagration and ash.

(v)

Like the residents of suburbia's web—Amoco Amoco—small chance
          for resurrection,
each bovine's face face down in creeks expressed mathematically—
          the way the letter π

has a lovely shape, has something like purpose—each cow each web
          each gas station,
black on pink, black on yellow, black on blue.

"You don't just say what you're saying in a poem."—Kim Hayes

First I saw an orange, a yellow, a blue, purple, and finally, red. I had
          my dukes up. I sat as if
in a tunnel and someone kept coming toward me and I kept duking him
          off. Then I was

on my mother's bed. I held her bones. My legs hurt and I wanted to
    kick so I did—
I kicked everyone and then I was up against my mother's snap
    and dissembling.

(vi)

I wrote a poem about a guy who sent me *Playboy*.

The stairs go up. The stairs go down.
I'm not sure why he picked me for his odd pedagogy.
I was seventeen, something called a co-ed.

He fancied himself old Henry Higgins.

I was seventeen, something called a co-ed.
I'm not sure why he picked me for his odd pedagogy.
The stairs go up. The stairs go down.

(vii)

I heard footsteps like dreaming, a vertigo of happenstance. The bullet
    in the back of the head
lodged like a Brussels sprout, a small velvet eggplant.

I was trampling on yellow tomatoes in the Ciccarella's garden, there
    was a baby with big
hair, an often invisible husband, and down the street, a building
    flanked by red bicycles.

It was on such a bicycle that a child named Dorothy came riding one day,
    and the baby,
soon to be spanked for the first time in her life by a mother chasing her
    wildly into the street,

fell in love, fell in love with red.

A GLOSSARY OF FOG

Silvertail—Insect that appears in fog and makes it beautiful.
Baba Ghanouj—Mediterranean mixture of garbanzo beans
      and fog.

She crouched beside the marsh where the warblers would arrive
      in their yellow suits,
increasing the way someone who hears the sound of wind might,
      the way velocity

increases beside the stove where she is about to step—that small circle,
      that debt.
She strapped her back to a stump and every time the river washed
      over her

she stayed alive against the ground like Fay Wray.
Her heart was as red as a fontanel. Her voice hovered like a ghost
      above the river.

There is no curve here, she said, only the fog at right angles.
She blew from the kitchen in a puff of condensation.

There was a tree to prop herself against, the tree she named *Euphrates*,
      Queen of Fog.
The King of Fog—*Bear Mountain*. Fog thinning—*Bones of a woman*.

She walked straight into it as she would walk into heaven, if heaven
      were in the palms
of her hands, if her hands were big as barn doors and heaven
      were spelled *F-O-G*.

FAY WRAY

She drew portraits of dead outlaws on her kitchen walls.
They counseled her from their mustachioed mouths.

Coyotes and blackmailers.
Underpants and sheep.

Women are sometimes plucked from alleys.
Sometimes they step off the El, and boom (boom).

From sight, like Van Gogh.
From memory, like Gaugin.

(Every part of her burns and ferns.)
Concupiscence, clobber, little coy pen.

I was counting the breath of clams on the beach, she said.
Then I was sorry for mollusks, sorry for their short lives.

I was baking nothing larger than popovers.
After that I made cakes from scratch.

I was a robber woman before, I stole shoes for my children.
After that I became a woman involved in fatality.

I drove through the prairie at night and in the morning
I saw planets of grass doing nothing in the wind.

There was a wound in my left hand,
a fallen angel in a bottle.

I wrapped my hair in a bun and speared it with a pen.
I hibernated into closure. I built an ark.

I forecasted evil
and received a bullet.

I was not King Kong.
I was not and have never been Fay Wray.

INTERVIEW WITH BONNIE PARKER

(i)

I believe in those erotic doomy twos, off-rhyme, slant-rhyme, potent portals to the planet's potholes, the way love takes a woman and spins her like a .38. When he came to me at last, fingers throwing death to my middle like a sweet gun, shots to the spleen, I revolved heroically for seconds then went down. It was the moon in Leo and he was the same fire I was used to only no one was afraid of him yet. *Pisser Possum Clothesline POW.*

There's a mouse curled behind my third eye. She's not asleep, she merely smells of lint, too squeaky to scream, too tiny to tussle, she's a fetus, a fossil, a fixed point, an ostrich, a salamander. She's a crook, a criminal, a marmot kneading her paws into my brain, into the heart in the middle of my dazed and bedazzled brain.

My kitchen ceiling's painted red,
blood's rushing to my house's head.

I still believe in love but not your game-playing kind, all that sex and paraphernalia hidden beneath the surface like a map of veins. You can see the love I mean on the bloody ceiling, stuck there like blobs of meat or pieces of heart.

Time/space, virtue/sin. When I was eighteen I sat in his front seat, somewhere between girl and outlaw—he put his hands on my head and pushed me into the earth like a screw. He tilted my chin with his fingers and said: You are a pebble in the wind's shoe.

He said: Luck is all we have.

I said: And anagrams.

Luck and anagrams is all we have.

And villanelles.

Luck and anagrams and villanelles is all we have.

And Nabokov.

Luck and anagrams and villanelles and Nabokov is all we have.

And flecked birds.

Luck and anagrams and villanelles and Nabokov and flecked birds
is all we have.

And scalloped molds.

Luck and anagrams and villanelles and Nabokov and flecked birds
and scalloped molds is all we have.

And margaritas.

He said: Tequila

(ii)

I like your hat I said companionably, the way stars brush each other as they
die, their midriffs ablaze, their skirts ashy. The proper way of calling on a
woman is with your sins rolled up in newspaper and stuck under your arm.
Ten minutes to invoke a charm. I offered him the same size hat but in a different
color. *If you're smart you'll take it and the shoes to match. The shoes with your name
on the soles. Hocus pocus.*

It was after the weather changed that I almost dumped him from my
bedroom and slept alone—*hocus locus*—and there was a time—*locus pocus*—
for that, believe me, the blue of it, the blue the blue the blue the blue the
blue.

The way the lake looked along the moon, the way his hat bobbed across the
sand, the halo of it, the point where I realized no matter how close I got to
moonlight, I could never step into it.

Cream roses with blood points leaping into the hands of my heart.

I rode the blood to Louisiana, circled around the derailment where the
mountains were a loom of horizon. This is the way I like my country—
plains and crevasses, foothills, and the peaks of syllables. I was cold beside the
flying boy. His vest billowed out behind him and he moved forward like an
opera. His mouth was full of flowers.

QUESTIONS FOR AN OUTLAW

The world was of freight trains and whistles of departure, death
        by water and death by locomotion.

She wanted weather like a train and the wind suddenly sent the river
        West and it shivered and turned pewter like a gun barrel.

(It's so cold fog slips out from inside her.)

There is wind and the river's shivering gray, the river in its hilly
        Jell-O mold.

They buried her beside the river in full view of gods, trains,
        and mountain.

And everyone before her said daisy and everyone after her said daisy.
        She (and she was the only one) said: Aster.

Like a spiral of dust receiving a name like a name blowing
        down the mountain the tops of trees the forming of thunder,

a fire a punch to the child's head a punch to the ear a punch
        to the eardrum.

I held her as she flew away, glistening.

BIJOU

Calculate the latitude and the solitary angle at which she throws
        herself
against orange where the paint makes its boundaries,
        the flat of it, the dry obsessive.

In the same way the cheetah is born into the brain of a Sunday
        driver.

Once I lived near Sing Sing where the streets curved around
        the houses and the houses
curved back and that's where I had my last good brew.

You looked at me and said: You'd better swallow up (your knuckles
        white as a Russian's,
hair on end like David Bowie's).

Oh, abstractions are just abstract until they have an ache in them.
        (Dunn)

In Chicago: a small dog frozen on its side, its owner calling *Lu Lu*.
Four iced pigeons in a row.

This is not rhetorical, although pointing East.
Remember the stories of our ride home? The times we leaned
        and fumbled?

That Elvis was a Capricorn? That the soul is made of myrrh?

What did you do on New Year's Eve, she asks Elvis, who(m) she
        privately rolls her eyes at.

There are others in this swamp tapping messages on a holy day.

No joke, no small thing.

PELE

Here is the buzz, the lament, the horror of overturned hazmats
        and all the trickling fear
and yet July 4th comes to Albuquerque the same way it comes
        to Chicago, and the women

cook pigs and hens and everywhere, the smell of slaughter.

As if they might slip off Acoma and be caught by a Franciscan
        priest which would make
them lucky citizens and him a hero.

Sarah thought as they approached the table's edge munching fry
        bread and pumpkin cookies:

There is the bone goddess and the corn goddess and the goddess
        who dwells on the mesa.

She tried to find the volcanoes but kept not finding them as they
        would mirage
then disappear as she got close.

The earth flumes and speeds, moves in a glut of non-ego, non-
        movied beauty.

Rinconada, Boca Negra, the glass dump at the base of the volcanoes
where bats kept missing them in the near-dark.

Elmer said anger is a waste of time, it only made him hoarse in 1970,
        Alcatraz,
when he was brave and young.

He said that if America hadn't used Navajo in WWII we'd all be
        speaking Japanese right
now and added it was a good thing we dropped the bombs.

She wondered if he might be testing her,
or if his anger had turned to fossil and mummy and petroglyph.

Her body sweat in unusual places, cant and vinegar, that poison
what's-its-name.

Wherever she walked: lava.

RIDING HOOD

A girl lay by the turnstiles with a bloody neck. We were surprised and quiet. Some of us calculated angles, distance from the turnstiles, her height times the number of feet it took to fall. We looked for a bump on the forehead, we searched the small clump of mourners for a mother or grandmother. Suddenly the girl rose from concrete and flew above us to the top of the station. She didn't stop to answer our questions. We said, They'd never pick her up like that if she weren't dead. She didn't blink an eye.

In the painting where Riding Hood floats above the forest floor holding the wolf's kind paw, I see two reflections in the blue pool and they both have ears and snout. This reminds me of reasons to keep myself in the city, my body disguised in a warm coat. I have nothing to offer the wolf, it's true, I haven't even a living grandmother, but the body belongs with other like bodies, and Red Riding Hood or not, I am a trespasser and these little creatures are the ones who belong: snake, owl, snail. The wolf is the man shouting near the El tracks, bouncing a ball so hard I hear it and weep. Let me live, I say, and he will because he carries no malice inside him—which is odd, I think, in this day, this age, on this green and leafy street.

Once I touched a dying woman. She could not be touched in the conventional way. I stood at her feet—she looked nothing like she had in her other life—and I touched her beyond her skin where she was already dying into, where no one could touch her but me.

Let's take our wombs and hide them in the sunflower fields.

Oh night flighter, oh scrumptious fatigue.

THE REALM OF THE WIDE

(i)

Every time I land a word, it loses cells and runs a temperature. You could jump the fire and ride to where the words are backdrafting. Feel yourself mingle with the word you love beside you. The way it moves, a delicate fish, a purple cut-out of a delicate fish, a shadow of a cut-out of a fish, salty sex.

The word: Outlandish.

She stands on the cliff and her head whirs like a halo, a terrible needle, the spin of a bird in the bush, extravagant as a newborn, expensive as the fare to far-off places like Hempstead, New York.

Firefighter, cop, Trojan horse. The elevator climbs to the top of the Sears Tower in three minutes flat although no one counts or maybe a certain person whose mind is always ticking might count, a person in love with beats or time. If everything could be a brief slice of bluefish on a plate. But this moon has got me up the way someone comes in and drags you out of bed to play cards or eat mayonnaise on toast at 3 AM or dance with her dance with her.

(ii)

- baby pigs
- distracted father
- long bungee cord attached to car
- clown nose and glasses
- a shaman in a wheelchair

There were baby pigs of all sizes from a couple of inches to a few pounds feeding on piles of scraps. Dad drove a long car with a bungee cord attached to the back in order to extricate his children from some (or the) danger. However, when it was my turn, he forgot I was there and started driving very fast around impossible suburbs. Then there was the old married couple who reminded me of the couple in *The Reluctant Shaman*. He was in a wheelchair and handed me his clown nose and glasses and then it was my turn to sit in the wheelchair and wear the clown nose and glasses. I can't remember if people could tell us apart or not. It mattered, but only slightly.

(iii)

The door opens, you are white-toweled from a spilt childhood, the blue spiral child in the deep clogged pool. We discovered the depth was a certain attainable depth, crispy with the leaf surface, and below that a concrete sky. Once a boy chased me with a BB gun. He was a summer boy named Ricky. I was ashamed that he'd aimed for my butt and hit it.

(iv)

Sorrowful _____

Joyful _____

Glorious _____.

Roll them around like hard candy, slang and tangle, peak and slide—the spontaneous combustion of the orange of the words, the crunch and smack, fossil and pictograph, a whole dam of rocks, stones, and words.

Many travelers choose to make a voyage to the Blessed Realms of the West in a small boat, there to encounter many tests, challenges and changes. They often take these voyages seemingly by accident; they become exiled from their own land, and enter the realm of the wide and trackless sea. (The heated stones themselves go into and come out of the water.)

(v)

She chopped all the heads off Mary in Joliet then came to Chicago to study art. It was like this before I met her, the baseball bats, the small heads rolling across lawns and mangers. Mâché brains scattered like seed, that smirk of conception, that maculate homespun Mom.

No sound no food no bells at midday no distance between the soul and the skin closing smooth and fast no space no small deceit nothing between the two like skull and brain.

24

"People who look for symbolic meanings fail to grasp the inherent mystery of the image. No doubt they sense this mystery, but they wish to get rid of it."—Rene Magritte

"Vanilla is the purest form of truth."—Nick

HE CROSSED THE HALLWAY WITH A SOUL IN HIS HAND

(i)

There was a prairie falcon, a boy with a rifle

There was a girl without defense, a line of scars along her spine

There was a circle of scalpels on her belly, a constellation above
     the field

There was a Pisces moon buried in dirt, a cistern settling

There was clean-smelling chaos, a kind of marital forlorn-ness

There was a solo sailor's glee, an eyepatch in the forest

There was a vision sweeping the barn, a gang of donuts

There was a particular hole, a child in loamy isolation

There was a fire-lit family, an ailing frog among the foxgloves

There was an oil spill on the ceiling, thunderous caregiving

There was quiet abandonment, a line of scars settling

There was an ailing circle of scalpels, a solo sailor in chaos

There was a kind of marital donut, a particular isolation

There was a gang buried in dirt, loamy caregiving

There was a child sweeping the barn, neglect among the foxgloves

There was a fire-lit forlorn-ness, a Pisces moon on her belly

There was a constellation without defense, an oil-spill above
     the field

There was a thunderous frog, a girl on the ceiling

There was a vision along her spine, a prairie falcon with a rifle

There was

There was

(ii)

Darkness down the driveway, darkness along the road
A woman eating chocolate, a man watching sports

Spine to the top of skull to the top of hair
Moving now across the page like the opposite of stone

I got to the end of the driveway where I could reach into darkness
It seemed that I could close my hands around Orion

There was a creepy stillness like bible verses
The woods were haunted by psalms

A man crossed the hallway with a soul in his hand
He got to the end where he could reach into darkness

TOY WEATHER

I went out on a night of weather and expected it to graze me but it was quiet behind the stone lion, delicate in its misadventures, that silly bee, that soul stealer.

The night of lightning

I had to make a decision fast, like taking control of a migraine, so a friend told me about the time lightning went straight through her walls and blew out everything from TV to furnace to back again. Luck was turning in the cyclones of air around the lakefront. Eden is a chaotic place, I thought, and the weatherman said my prediction was correct but only for forty-eight hours.

Is weather free at any time to change directions?

What would prompt it to change stories within directions?

Should I think of weather as six to eight ongoing simultaneous stories?

Can stories be any length?

Sarah and I ate outside and the wind blew as if we were Joan of Arc, sudden and informed by cold presences with voices unlike our own yet simple, and the South Side man said Just like That because the temp had fallen at least five degrees due to nothing we'd seen except our hair blasted to the East and green umbrellas threatening and the legs of all the walkers suddenly spirited in the way of seekers of something extraordinary: a cloud opening or a window flying from a building or everyone so good at loving even the most frightened is still.

Can weather, by some Glamour, change men into beasts?

What is the source of the increase of works of weather?

Can weather be generated by incubi and succubi?

How is weather transported from place to place?

There is more weather now the jolly girls say but the girls of doom say—sail on to the front of the lake, the gloomy trees beside the lagoon, the turtles skipping over the pond like stones from a child's hand.

The brown suitcase

The suitcase holds something close to weather but doesn't move when I pick it up. The handle sticks to my hand as if it wants something. There is an ache in me to carry it away but I won't. The woman who left the suitcase is no longer here. Her cat is missing too, a small tiger roaming the woods around the suitcase. There is a wide circle around the suitcase, a cat within it stalking angles, the diameter of the circle sliding across the suitcase like any other line: to Hutchinson Island, to Albuquerque—the circumference of the circle divided by the diameter, an irrational number that goes on and on like the weather inside the suitcase.

3.14159265358979323846264338327950288419716939937510582097494
45923078...

There are 6.4 billion known digits in pi.

It would take 33 years with no coffee or sleep to recite them all.

Lichen on black oak.

Sands of a glacier lake.

There was a girl with pieces of star all over her. She sat in the middle of the lake, something of the lake or for the lake. I saw her stuck in a lily's legs and said: Your suitcase waits in a room with walls like a book. There was nothing else to say so I hooked her and reeled her in like a wide-mouthed bass.

The night of the wide-mouthed bass

The man from down the road caught a small fish and called to me in my cabin. He was a good man, you could tell, but he skinned and filleted the poor live thing right there on my picnic table with the knife I'd brought from home. I love the way shadows move on the trees that bend over the lake. That one, that white birch, sounds like taffeta.

Here is the green porch with its thermometer rising.

On the floor of the forest—the weather of ghosts.

Ghosts inhabit forests no more no less than rivers.

Weather hurts my ears with its acoustics.

Ghosts run right through me and keep running—down to the river for a drink, up a hollow tree. Touched like this, I am nevertheless clothed and breathing, opaque and pounding with blood—and when the ghosts hang their slips in the black oaks I call out. Leaves float down and cover my feet. Ghosts sit in the trees videotaping. Spiders spin lace around my breasts.

π

3.14159265358979323846264338327950288419716939937510582097494459230781640628620899862803482534211706
79...

Drones (impregnate) that stings that is all they do is drones is ouch all queens all drones they drones ouch stings do they do stings drones drones ouch drones they queens all is hives they ouch ouch stings that all queens that do all drones all all drones queens is that hives is ouch they hives all queens stings all stings stings is all they drones hives queens ouch that do stings hives do they ouch do they hives ouch all all ouch do they ouch hives drones stings ouch they is drones stings they that that queens hives do queens all...

THE GIRLS OF DOOM

"… they were dancin' all over the room."—Gary U.S. Bonds

Pull your own roots and begin to climb. Sparrow, mosquito, a rush of vowels carved in stone. A sharpshooter in an uncivil peace.

Two couples climbed the stairs to the petroglyphs, talking in high and low voices, heading straight toward history. They said ach and then were quiet. A woman said, I hope it doesn't fall down, it's a big rock. You've seen one rock you've seen 'em all, a man said.

They scribbled their names over three-thousand-year-old carvings:

A.V. Dean   Charles Caron
NY

The girl who left the concrete suitcase at the top of the subway stairs said I'm on my way home to where the river divides the twins and the people shine like robots. The suitcase cracked three times—loud whip in a reality of roots and dirt, a yin of gravity, a surrender of concrete to coyote.

When a girl thinks alone, she thinks evil.

The flow of girls begins to misbehave.

The girls appeared, then chaos—and then, ephemeral in their
     instability,

the girls swirled above the table like spun glass, all blazed.

       She took speed in school like everyone else. Nevertheless, she slept and remained silent. Someone said this was because she behaved badly around drugs. True, she replied, remembering that she almost died at six and there in the hospital had become a bionic child capable of placing her hand in fire and, although burned, she never fled.

Here is a blowing absolutely like glazed fire. Hot glass and glory hole. Glass in hues, making wings. Flame blue glass orange, dipping into glory then dipping. Neck stretching. Straight into the glass's mouth. He said, which came first, the water or the fire? Nothing is perfect in glass-blowing, except tonight the weather, he said.

In the middle of the meadow, a girl struck by lightning.

Head full of lagoon like a girl treading water.

On the floor of the forest, the footprints of girls.

Girls run with their eyes slanted toward irrational numbers.

SENTENCING

(i)

The population next year is a function of the population this year.

Ideas that require people to reorganize their picture of the world
        provoke hostility.

Finally, death is a game of inches, the critical boundary between
        steadiness and oscillation.

(ii)

The women hovered above the pool engaged in discourse.

I asked them if they offered their newborn children to hailstorms
        and tempests.

How do devils enter a human body without doing any hurt, when
        they cause such
metamorphosis by means of prestidigitation, I asked.

My questions became less and less curious, more and more inquisitional.

(iii)

My mother refused to kill insects. She would allow my father to swat flies,
        that's it.
When she was too sick to stand, one of us would transport the bug
        outside without injury.

(iv)

—the first method of pronouncing sentence: when the accused is no more
        than defamed
—the second method of sentencing: the case of one accused upon a light
        suspicion
—the third manner of sentence: the case of one accused upon a
        strong suspicion
—the fourth kind of sentence: the case of one who is gravely suspect

—the method of passing sentence upon one who is both suspect and
 defamed
—the method of passing sentence upon one who hath confessed to heresy,
 but is not penitent
—the method of passing sentence upon one who hath confessed to heresy
 but is relapsed, albeit now penitent
—the method of passing sentence upon one who hath confessed to heresy
 but is impenitent, although not relapsed
—of one who has confessed to heresy, is relapsed, and is also impenitent
—of one taken and convicted, but denying everything
—of the method of passing sentence upon one who has been accused by
 another, who has been or is to be burned at the stake
—of the method of passing sentence upon one who annuls spells; and of
 midwives and Arch-Wizards
—Finally, the method of passing sentence upon those who enter or cause to
 be entered an appeal, whether such be frivolous or legitimate and
 just

(v)

A total of 113 species of ants is recorded by county from the state
 of Illinois.

Ten species represent new state records.

Hecate is the best symbol of death and rebirth we've got, yet
 most of us can't stand to look at her.

Ants can eat an entire person in less time than an oil change.

(vi)

The women walked willy-nilly across the land.

The earth swallowed them up.

TURTLE BEACH

From this poxed plot steaming with zebras and one-eyed moths,
dapple of cabbage palm, whine of saw palmetto,

your sedated hair falls without fanfare into the Atlantic—
God-ball, lens of no mercy, sweet unnerving head.

(Your Mother of Pearl skin, your flash of a beach trip,
kelpy sea-breath eating me as you are eaten.)

There are no edible fish in the St. Lucie—rot and contusion,
Saab and Cadillac. Overflow from Okeechobee flavors them

with blood. Bump bump bump of cars on the causeway.
And yet I gather the purple scallops you said

were very rare, gorge myself on sickly mullet
lemoned and breaded to hide their vacuous bruises, their

gory gills. My wishes hiss in the mouths of slugs,
delinquencies hush, endings seem unfathomedly undeserved.

Everything in the way of you sludges back to sea,
green-foamed and ghostly as the mother loggerhead who

bolts with blessed little memory of treachery or offspring.

ST. LUCIE

She threw her hand over the back of the seat and light
flew from her fingers out the window where she sat spotting alligators.

She voted for weather that was paunchy and country,
unused as she was to the air of women and certain crossroads,

fatality of tea steaming cozy and lethal, masterplots
made to create illusions with a hint of rib thrown in.

Colors of skim-milk and teeth—was that always the way?
A terribly one-sided signature?

She'd often thought snow insinuated itself and lollopped from porch
        eaves
down and down the way of stairs and she assumed God

had created it for her. "For me," she'd said in surprise, a simple child,
        barely
fierce enough to recognize back-breaking duplicity when she saw it.

Nothing in the century to appease or otherwise blither.
The whole universe parceled in a bite, a bit, a certain length, width,
        fragrance,

so zoological the tongue aches, the way it eases delicacies,
the celebrated and misshapen distances between words.

Her hair's no longer symmetrical, breasts are free, nightsticks &
        bibles—
what cruiser?—what results?

She's closer to dumb than a thumb of valerian.
Her hair hums on the causeway.

THE POSSIBLE

12:35

The child fell into the sea, searching for the hatch in the phosphorescence. She smiled in the dark, a halved moon, the reason Lilith said to Eve, "You need sun, my lamb, you need color in your sepulchral visage, darling." I had a friend who called me darling. She wrote letters and started them darling with an *h, dahling.* It was during this time I decided the word was good for our souls.

1:03

Last night at She She Café we were surrounded by hairdressers—beautiful hair, good bodies, the owner rich as cream. He handed out his salon's cards to all the restaurant patrons. Then he presented a large penis cake to the birthday man. It was this show of affection that made me cry as I read about the things I can and cannot have. *It was the ocean I wanted, waves like pets.*

12:56

I was reminded of Father Steven, who long ago saved my life (if not my soul). I saw him a few years later at a home for wayward priests. He appeared chubbily from around a corner (what was I doing there?) and recognized me as the woman he'd turned into a pagan. Consider the apple tree heavy with fruit, he counseled, how silky the skin of the boa.

12:41

Someone coming to the back door, pressing the broken buzzer. Now the woman breathes as she stretches, her clothes go swoosh swoosh, her soft and singular indrawn breath improvises reality. I'd like to go upstairs, she says. Let's go: upstairs. Take another breath.

WORM REEF

The performance artist from Miami did amazing things with nightcrawlers. She put them between her toes and wiggled them. She took them for a ride on a little train. She dropped them down the front of her dress until, after some time, they fell out on the floor. I remember how I saw her crying in a back room saying she had forgotten a whole section of the performance. I wanted to tell her it had been perfect just the way it was.

The family that fled in this flimsy raft has disappeared at sea. Their belongings have been placed on a small table, exhibited without pomp on the porch of the House of Refuge. A child's sneaker, rosary beads, a rusty can of beans. Knowing little of Gulf Stream or treacherous reefs, I too might have thrown some essentials onto a balloon boat and set sail for Florida with my loved ones. It's beautiful here and I would have had little to lose.

I fear the spiral of the death nugget, the sweet well, the seep of mine filth, its blame and thunder. You'll find me pining near the silky worm. (Sarah said, as I caressed the tiny white creature, "Sorry to say but that's a maggot.") I fear the winding guts deliberate in the fishy pail. The bank of sound louder than a thousand gulls. (She said, "*I'm* frightened, how 'bout you?") The suspended time of open green. A minute, ten, you can count the bodies in the time it takes to row the same patch over and over in hurricane dark. We were sound asleep, then jumping into sea—it held us down as if we should pray to it. I heard the small raft whistle by then catch me on the back of the neck where moments before she'd kissed me.

TOY WEATHER 2

Once upon a time, at some time in history, either ancient or recent, there was a hamster, a fuzzy rodent, in a bag of potato chips, Ruffles, on the coffee table, cocktail table, beside the tennis racket, the webbed implement used for a popular net game, which the sitcom star, the one listed in the credits, picked up, chose and lifted, and whacked, pummeled, the hamster, fuzzy rodent, with, although it wasn't truly, really, a hamster, fuzzy rodent, and certainly, positively, he, the male of the species, was no star, not even a twinkle.

I see shoes big as Paraguay.
I hear throats clear, someone in the hall swish past, saying um.
I taste my fear.
I smell my sneeze.
I touch.
I feel the way lightning would if it created me.

Surely, I said, you were born into a body that would abandon you at twelve, keep on until raped at twenty-three, then open twice on a Sunday five years apart, jetting new bodies into old men's hands.

Love, M

I wish I could create a story. 12:32 and the clouds are covering the blue.

I adore the idea of _____.
I think about _____ all the time.

If it's true, as they say, that man's convulsions go on building endless layers of fossils, then I shall love you until we find ourselves rotting in sand, our membranes sticky and soapy and gangrenous as we melt into stone, into each other in a way we dreamed, something like the stickiness we find ourselves in right now, my dilettante.

The magnolia tree is perfect, a perfect shape of tree. The dead trees around it moan and fall over each other.

Batman, you are bigger than a palm tree. You are Egyptian with your ears and gold belt. The sea laps your thighs, Batman, look at how long your gloves are. You could lick a cloud you're so tall. No one is scared of you. Everyone cruises along in a pleasure boat beside you. When you finish your tale they all laugh. Ha ha, Batman, they say, ha ha.

Barometer holds.

Peak up perk down the strings the shtrings make believe you love me
    like

this. Inched into the blue the soul poof!—she's back and I'm too
    through.

I feel red when I do magic.

12:46

Here I am pulling a wagon of fear. You could expose the word solder, a silent
"l," like a salmon before she runs, silly with generational desire. Gleaming
above the stream, silvery scale and spine.

On the red building there is a small simile with a dancer dancing in the red
like a tooth, the way a tooth would look if it could stand on one foot—if
it had a foot, if it had toes, toe shoes, music. I would lay the building on its
side and live there in the red, the red within the red, the place where free
the place where easy.

It was of no use because she was filled with popped brain cells, she was awful in her denial, she was caught in a backwash of forgetting.

Everything we said made sense on a beautiful day: bird, pink, conception. Our love was partially visible, the way we swatted shoulders or put on bracelets and earrings, were good to each other.

My hair is blowing so there must be wind. Zoe's on the cold ground, me on my jacket. My mother is buried in the same cemetery as Zoe's stalker's father. Someone stuck someone's urn and a statue of Mary right next to my mother's stone. Along the side of the cemetery are dozens of baby graves. Zoe just called us the Cemetery Sisters.

Here is the Cemetery Church:

little church

Keeping the head in the water the way a fish would, not above, always cutting through liquid, moving side to side—cutting across the lake—diagonal—like Lincoln or Milwaukee or Clark—you can make it to Michigan this way, you can almost keep going if you've filled your belly—to New York—New York.

We borrowed stones from the chaos of the lake from the lake the fish surprised us, skeleton and skull with the half-eaten eye—the running down the dune. Falling into the pink house where no music but in us. Hooking ourselves with glow worms, adverbs, tongue and tongue. Falling in the pink, falling into the pink house, the fish we devoured and left in bones on the shore.

EATING FLORIDA

Like the tongue in the tunnel of my head, I had no weight, no
    necessary arc.
I said a noise close to *wah wah wah*.

Snook and grouper fell sick simultaneously, lavender sores
    gleamed.
Anglers drowned in sudden holes, coolers tied to their legs with
    hemp.

Raccoons swiped turtle eggs, panthers swallowed raccoons,
    humans poached panthers,
battalions of predators devoured my mother's ribs, one by one.

During her last rites the communion wafer stuck to the roof of my
    mouth while
her lips smacked hungrily. I said: The ocean invented that sound.

When the moon sliced Pisces, a woman jumped from the top
    of a nearby building
although there was a husband sleeping and children dreaming
    behind her.

For the women who died here, for their breath that creates the fog,
    for the ulcers
on the fishes' eyes, for the need to believe it won't be me, it won't
    be me,

it won't be my daughters. Even Godzilla, who rises from Atlantis
    in an ecstasy of fire,
stomping sunbathers, fracturing boardwalks, even he looks
    bewildered—

the beginnings of melanoma, the pious glaze of death.

TOY WEATHER 3

Here is the storm in the star in the stars in the stars that were there the moment you were born, your blood a streak in the night's iris.

And the hurricane they named Gordon, his tail end, mallards hunching on the sea wall. Zoe swears the palm trees are Confederate soldiers who stare at her and whisper, the way people think they own these squalls, the way the wind pushes in like a developer. In the basket: pieces of sand dollars from Turtle Beach, their intricacies devastating and chaotic, commotion of the gods of sea, air, and palms.

It came from the East as always and trampled the rooftops, that sticky wind that wet-eyed salutation. The rains flew so hard, banking horizontal across the turnpike, the Chevy shuddered then stopped in mid-air like a herring gull. Dragonflies whooshed above the car—and those infinite others with the white guts pounded against my ruined windshield.

I thought: The dead are slippery lovers. They approach me in the morning with their sideburns showing. Or they repeat everything I say like a pesky sibling. *A pesky sibling.* I need something tame to flirt at my window, a lion or a scorpion, not a mean-spirited hurricane, a bickering tornado.

You never know when you'll be asked to think out loud. Suddenly sound is made and/or required and you are not equal to it, here nor there, the day October yet summer and the day goes on, parts the air and sets up a sanctuary, a worn womb of sleep.

On the walls the saints dance in the shape of bells, the cross points to all four directions at once.

She said *clearly* as if her mind periodically erased slates and there it was: her own see-through universe. Voices and symbiosis. You want the end to come because it will be that relief, and as it comes, the ions grow more and negative, dense and stormy, like the twister in the photograph saying cheese or wheeze—and the air is not the air you grew up in, it's cinematic, this ending, this eviction, this paralyzing close, the jump approaching, the muscles in your neck snaking.

SHE SAT IN MY LAP LIKE A STONE

1. She flew into the burning maple beside the cupola and was
   gone.

2. Her face was a small face in the moon, a triangle bone.

3. She looked inside like looking into water.

4. A desert of teeth.

5. Her bones carried music to me from her life of dishes, cutlery,
   placemats.

6. She said, Your hands are always warm.

7. Stone in the mouth, stone in the tumbled sea.

8. The way a star reaches earth as a fig seed pointed downward.

9.

10. The children said: Your bones are beautiful, like the stalks of
    lilies.

11. A rainstick, a didgeridoo.

12. A protruding rib, a needle point

13. shitfuckpiss.

14. Her spine held together by light. Her bones buzzed delirium.

YOU'RE BABYLON AND I'M BRAZIL

Lately I live in the groupings I make with my eyes, the way I bestow
        too much fuel
on a particular landscape, the south side of a city, a project of calamitous
        elevation.

The trouble is the loose window with the mirror to the moon's surface,
        the glossy road
that reaches into cosmos's cool core and wrestles with metaphor.
        Everything I know

drifts into the scene before me, hummingbird and trumpet vine, the sun
        on one knee
beside the lagoon, water lilies gaping.

*

The ghost in the oyster shell is a fool of small places—molecules
        between people who write
like gourmands in the throes of food, like a pitfall, a sorry god, a last
        joint, a fulcrum,

an aviator, four score and one hundred Lilliputians ago. Words come
        when I'm obedient,
when the infamous thing about me is the way I part my hair.

There is a lake running with silver and in this lake are waves turning West
        turning South
where a woman lies, head down on a hill in Illinois. The lake gathers stones
        and stores them

in her treasures. How cliché you seem, says my mind, small girl holding
        no one's hand, blank

space in the air beside you. My body folds into itself and says:

There are lilies all over the lake, closed now, but ready, in hours, to
        break apart.

★

Keep going in the midst of ornery grasses and tall latitudes. If ants pull
          each other along
and counsel each other in the same way as these children spread on the
          lawn like

chenille, then when they're settled down for a night of tacos, unashamed
          and eating
strenuously, in fact, engaged in serious taco competition, it's time to enroll
          in a series

of movements regarding spontaneity, all you can eat stenciled down your
          legs, tattooed
on your palms, little hairs bursting from your pores like soldiers on a long
          beach.

When I was in Florida I missed the ivory woodpecker—no easy way to
          her cry, no
forwarding sound, not a beak, an egg, a soft and tiny shoe.

Repeat the gist and grit, the holy angles and digested grouper that slings
          into your being
from an ocean you've learned never to trust and in that certainty, trust it.
          Be certain

of the signs around you: ink, swan, drill of a woodpecker. Destroy
          the world.
It will fly out again from between your legs.

★

A horse gallops into the sound barrier creating a window into 4D, a time
          unlike now
but closer to now like the voices of painters, the stilled voices of birds.

The rage of a cardinal.

The scent of several men in lawn chairs exercising self.

A woman cried because a man said step on the cicada and everyone
        laughed. He didn't
step on the cicada and she didn't know the people well but he said that
        and they did that

and then she did what she did and I saw her in the circle suddenly so
        angry she could step
on the man so I said let's step on the man and we all laughed.

A mouse ran out and looked exactly like Mickey, the old Mickey of the
        early cartoons.
He had something white in his mouth and he stopped for a moment
        to be surprised

that I was there as quiet as I was (as a mouse) and then moved on.

Even when the answer involves a flow to the head a blow to the head,
        a cello. Now we round
the unbelievable curve before Sedgwick where the conductor slows
        to about ten mph or else.

I always wait for this place with a small fear like before penetration,
        that tiny held breath.

★

There are five minutes there are all the times flying into the corpse—
        we are too blah—we are
blah—write me again and this time smoke and stink and if I ever get loose
        I will pop

into a sun and you will dry away.

Read me into the phosphorous that's all over your legs, your arms, your
        gorgeous
green tongue, oh land, where is the land—ah oh! We are earth-bereft,
        we are fidgeters

in the propelled terra the way the earth whirs in orbit—in orbit—hear

that? Every time I say
orbit I get a pulse. You could call this nonsense, but why am I self-
conscious as a kangaroo,

absorbed as a sapphire? When I was young I loved *him* because I was
female and *her*
because I was female—and gender bound me in its usual expected ways.

If I stop talking everything will be white space and I will age into it like
peacock blue ink.
As children we were given blue-black, humblest of all the inks,
a student's ink, but my

fingers ached for peacock blue. When Ntozake appeared in Chicago she
said people die
from lack of beauty. I thought of you and lathered henna into my hair
and painted my nipples

peacock blue.

*

We are all the time squeezing into the lines all the time yellowing. Here
is the green paper.
Here are the squares upon it and the boys swigging in the classroom like
rampant sycamores.

I saw a sycamore once. A Bronx point of interest I called Twins. She was
split at the base
and spired in two directions, much like you and I and the way we
started out before we flew

in a vee toward sky.

The way the shaking takes us down. And the birds say. And the birds say.
Increase, beautiful,
there are twin trees everywhere but none as old as the one they call
Twins in the Bronx.

What if you end up alone you say. Then you will be like me, I say, then

you will be like me,
a half smile. I want to go away from you and today I said it. Tunnel.
        Pointillism. Someone

smarter than me at something. Bring the babies around the pool. Behave
        among them.
The ghosts are enough to break me into a thousand tunnels.

★

I wish my name were Zelda. I wish I were a filmmaker. When all of me
        collides with all
of you will I be too busy? I just missed being killed by a huge window that
        flew

off the red skyscraper and sliced a woman in half under the awning of a
        pizzeria.
Peter Greenaway, watch over me.

There's a story about a woman who was stepping on a manhole cover
        when it blew her
sky-high. I fear that word, sky-high. It reminds me of how air is for sale
        in the city, how lives

develop like cones into the heavens. How much for a fourteenth floor,
        a twenty-ninth?
How much for a cubic foot of space, cloud caught in an air-shaft, how
        much would you pay

to shake hands with the sun? Put 'er there, I've heard people say as they
        hold out their hands.
Put 'er there, pardner.

We could meet in Albuquerque. If it's just sex, we could have it in the
        desert where cactus
survive without water but we'll have to be careful—remember how
        dehydrated we got

under all those quilts? Now an old-spice smelling coffee-smelling man
        has sat beside me

and said oh shoot out loud as if the world might care about him.

★

Sex is a trick, a letting go in such a way that you're always there. A trick
        the body and mind
play together, a play, a collaboration. The body dives while the mind
        holds the rope although

it might be the other way, the mind hang-gliding, the body back on the
        cliff taking notes.

You can pull back on the strings of civilization, striate into the dung-
        covered statue of Mary,
Mother of Le Roy, or non-comprehend all of the above. It doesn't matter.
        Time is a lake. I'm

in the boat not rowing. Last night when we walked from the Biograph,
        a young man waved
from inside a ginmill. You talked to me of denial and I nodded. He drank
        a tall beer and I

nodded at you and I nodded at him. Think of the word NOD until it
        becomes a sound
in the corner of your mouth. Swallow it. Digest.

If I leave something out will the way I didn't use the word NOD truly
        raise that woman
back to life? If I continue toward NOD will the dog bite take its place
        in your life's utility,

the same way as Alanis Morissette sings, whiny but beautiful, pathetic
        but simmering,
causing my throat to close. Yesterday your body said, tell, don't show.

I threw my secrets at you just to see you nod.

★

12:04   The pith the wax the string the break the fuel the post the posit the reach.

12:06   A word a point a pout a puss. Increasing clouds. One and a half, stop, one and a half.

12:08   We are forming against the Republic, we are debting, we are dead.

12:12   Bargains hit us—Bim Bam Bop. With an egg on top.

12:14   Pukka pukka pukka pukka.

12:15   A woman died, creating a hole in the sky, or so it seems.

★

She she she she she and she she she and she over and into on through the
        dance the spouse
a dilemma. The priestess and the pallbearer, the home run, the home,
        my running home

to bread to the sink the splish the grease the sponge. She and squeeze
        and squeeze the trough
the mate the sorted the sorter the sortie the béchamel the hollandaise
        the reverence we hold.

There were fire engines, ambulances, police cars. A body on the sidewalk.

Creating an orbit around herself, she solemnly dreamed never to glow
        the way she had
at birth. In this way, the pupils of her eyes blackened and smoked. It was in
        the dream

to poke fun at reverence—and a couple she knew well—a Florida couple
        —reached up
from the floor beside her bed and grabbed her. Only once before had
        someone truly

touched her in a dream. She'd slipped from her bed on Bernard Street
        and someone
hoisted her back up, a great hand lifted her back into her dream where
        colors

of spilled blood ran Kodak and satisfying, smearing her whole waking day
        with hope.

★

I will walk into Wonderland with which I've been in love since childhood.
        Blue-black
or peacock blue? I don't believe in symbols—portents, yes, I like to predict.
        I can be honest

about anything, just give me enough ink. Alice is right: Sometimes we
        want meaning: My
daughter's ear. My daughter's hands. My father's hands. My brother's
        heart. My sister's hands.

My father's ear.

A look at chaos shows this to be true. Here we are, three bodies colliding.
        I am the one
ejected because of my light weight and my ability to orgasm. There is
        nothing left of me,

except as vehicle or inspiration, in your nightly plot. Still, I think about
        the atom and the way
electrons tunnel into new places with a sweet intelligence. Must
        everything relate to me,

even something as small as a leap?

★

We're here in the tunnel again. The tunnel has sides like a brain, bumpy
        and soft. If I punch

the tunnel it springs back, unalarmed, the way I would like a parent to be.

I wonder if it's the devil who has me, if that's why life is so burning bizarre.
     Or maybe
you could lift me up and throw me down a hundred times and every time
     I break there are

more of me, holograms with little legs, running around the world objecting
     to things.

★

Swing me into tomorrow like a lantern.

Place me solidly, a small sack of sand with a candle burning, on the ground.

You're Babylon and I'm Brazil. Big words on the tongue, open flame.
     The window flew
from the 29th floor splitting the woman in half. There she was, lovely
     ghost preparing

to lift off. There was her child on the sidewalk pulling her mother's skirt.
     I was walking
South in the city and you were home not knowing how close I'd come
     to glass, how Brazil

I'd felt as I Babyloned down Wabash, as I brushed the beveled edge
     and walked away.

VENUS EXAMINES HER BREAST

She's pissed at all the minor milk ducts
flaring in her one remaining breast. Oh

shit, she says, and sets her chin
as ages flip in mock somnambulism, too

lean of mind to expect much from a goddess.
Oh stadiums of light, oh babble.

Aspiration takes seconds, the lump
a syringe of cloudy lemon soup. Look,

says the Doc, Now aren't we a happy camper?
Venus packs her tools for Rome where

everything is so expensive yet familiar.
She poses and sculpts in turn, naked

as a snake-shaped scar, chipping slowly
at 17th century stone. Nothing

gets better than this, she thinks: Nipple,
lymph glands, bowling arm flexed

to capacity. I can shift out of first!
Making love, she reminds herself to stay

anchored in the mirrored now. You're
gorgeous, she says, flushing, leaning in.

NOTES

I've borrowed [in "Red (vi)," and "She Sat in My Lap Like a Stone"] from the craft of poets Gregg Shapiro and Sue Kwock Kim, respectively; and sparingly, in other poems, from the texts of Annie Dillard (*For the Time Being*, 2000), James Gleick (*Chaos: Making a New Science*, 1987), Heinrich Kramer and James Spreger (*Malleus Maleficarum,* 1486), Sylvia Plath (*Ariel*, 1961), and Barbara Ras (*Bite Every Sorrow*, 1998).

★

Inexpressible gratitude to Gerry Luke (in memory) & Gillian for hospice; to FPS & family; to Connie & John, Harriet & her cuzzes, & all the folks at Ox-Bow for breathtaking space/time; to the *Red-Heads*—Alice, Cin, Kim, Sharon, & Susen for adventures; to Lori and Terese for great reads; to Cobalt, Denise, Linda B., Marilyn H., Nick C., Valerie & Zoe for holding my place; to Jennifer & Emily for daughtering; and to Sarah for constantly landing on my roof.

PREVIOUS TITLES IN THE CARNEGIE MELLON POETRY SERIES

1988
Preparing to Be Happy, T. Alan Broughton
Red Letter Days, Mekeel McBride
The Abandoned Country, Thomas Rabbitt
The Book of Knowledge, Dara Wier
Changing the Name to Ochester, Ed Ochester
Weaving the Sheets, Judith Root

1989
Recital in a Private Home, Eve Shelnutt
A Walled Garden, Michael Cuddihy
The Age of Krypton, Carol J. Pierman
Land That Wasn't Ours, David Keller
Stations, Jay Meek
The Common Summer: New and Selected Poems, Robert Wallace
The Burden Lifters, Michael Waters
Falling Deeply into America, Gregory Djanikian
Entry in an Unknown Hand, Franz Wright

1990
Why the River Disappears, Marcia Southwick
Staying Up For Love, Leslie Adrienne Miller
Dreamer, Primus St. John

1991
Permanent Change, John Skoyles
Clackamas, Gary Gildner
Tall Stranger, Gillian Conoley
The Gathering of My Name, Cornelius Eady
A Dog in the Lifeboat, Joyce Peseroff
Raised Underground, Renate Wood
Divorce: A Romance, Paula Rankin

1992
Modern Ocean, James Harms
The Astonished Hours, Peter Cooley
You Won't Remember This, Michael Dennis Browne
Twenty Colors, Elizabeth Kirschner
First A Long Hesitation, Eve Shelnutt
Bountiful, Michael Waters

Blue for the Plough, Dara Wier
All That Heat in a Cold Sky, Elizabeth Libbey

1993
Trumpeter, Jeannine Savard
Cuba, Ricardo Pau-Llosa
The Night World and the Word Night, Franz Wright
The Book of Complaints, Richard Katrovas

1994
If Winter Come: Collected Poems, 1967–1992, Alvin Aubert
Of Desire and Disorder, Wayne Dodd
Ungodliness, Leslie Adrienne Miller
Rain, Henry Carlile
Windows, Jay Meek
A Handful of Bees, Dzvinia Orlowsky

1995
Germany, Caroline Finkelstein
Housekeeping in a Dream, Laura Kasischke
About Distance, Gregory Djanikian
Wind of the White Dresses, Mekeel McBride
Above the Tree Line, Kathy Mangan
In the Country of Elegies, T. Alan Broughton
Scenes from the Light Years, Anne C. Bromley
Quartet, Angela Ball
Rorschach Test, Franz Wright

1996
Back Roads, Patricia Henley
Dyer's Thistle, Peter Balakian
Beckon, Gillian Conoley
The Parable of Fire, James Reiss
Cold Pluto, Mary Ruefle
Orders of Affection, Arthur Smith
Colander, Michael McFee

1997
Growing Darkness, Growing Light, Jean Valentine
Selected Poems, 1965-1995, Michael Dennis Browne
Your Rightful Childhood: New and Selected Poems, Paula Rankin
Headlands: New and Selected Poems, Jay Meek
Soul Train, Allison Joseph

The Autobiography of a Jukebox, Cornelius Eady
The Patience of the Cloud Photographer, Elizabeth Holmes
Madly in Love, Aliki Barnstone
An Octave Above Thunder: New and Selected Poems, Carol Muske

1998
Yesterday Had a Man In It, Leslie Adrienne Miller
Definition of the Soul, John Skoyles
Dithyrambs, Richard Katrovas
Postal Routes, Elizabeth Kirschner
The Blue Salvages, Wayne Dodd
The Joy Addict, James Harms
Clemency and Other Poems, Colette Inez
Scattering the Ashes, Jeff Friedman
Sacred Conversations, Peter Cooley
Life Among the Trolls, Maura Stanton

1999
Justice, Caroline Finkelstein
Edge of House, Dzvinia Orlowsky
A Thousand Friends of Rain: New and Selected Poems, 1976-1998, Kim
Stafford
The Devil's Child, Fleda Brown Jackson
World as Dictionary, Jesse Lee Kercheval
Vereda Tropical, Ricardo Pau-Llosa
The Museum of the Revolution, Angela Ball
Our Master Plan, Dara Wier

2000
Small Boat with Oars of Different Size, Thom Ward
Post Meridian, Mary Ruefle
Hierarchies of Rue, Roger Sauls
Constant Longing, Dennis Sampson
Mortal Education, Joyce Peseroff
How Things Are, James Richardson
Years Later, Gregory Djanikian
On the Waterbed They Sank to Their Own Levels, Sarah Rosenblatt
Blue Jesus, Jim Daniels
Winter Morning Walks: 100 Postcards to Jim Harrison, Ted Kooser

2001
The Deepest Part of the River, Mekeel McBride
The Origin of Green, T. Alan Broughton

Day Moon, Jon Anderson
Glacier Wine, Maura Stanton
Earthly, Michael McFee
Lovers in the Used World, Gillian Conoley
Sex Lives of the Poor and Obscure, David Schloss
Voyages in English, Dara Wier
Quarters, James Harms
Mastodon, 80% Complete, Jonathan Johnson
Ten Thousand Good Mornings, James Reiss
The World's Last Night, Margot Schilpp

2002
Astronaut, Brian Henry
Among the Musk Ox People, Mary Ruefle
The Finger Bone, Kevin Prufer
Keeping Time, Suzanne Cleary
Fromt he Book of Changes, Stephen Tapscott
What it Wasn't, Laura Kasischke
The Late World, Arthur Smith
Slow Risen Among the Smoke Trees, Elizabeth Kirschner

2003
Imitation of Life, Allison Joseph
A Place Made of Starlight, Peter Cooley
The Mastery Impulse, Ricardo Pau-Llosa
Except for One Obscene Brushstroke, Dzvinia Orlowsky
Taking Down the Angel, Jeff Friedman
Casino of the Sun, Jerry Williams
Trouble, Mary Baine Campbell
Lives of Water, John Hoppenthaler

2004
Freeways and Aqueducts, James Harms
Tristimania, Mary Ruefle
Prague Winter, Richard Katrovas
Venus Examines Her Breast, Maureen Seaton
Trains in Winter, Jay Meek
The Women Who Loved Elvis All Their Lives, Fleda Brown
The Chronic Liar Buys a Canary, Elizabeth Edwards
Various Orbits, Thom Ward